OF SINGLES AND DOUBLES

ROSALIE MOORE

OF SINGLES AND DOUBLES

WOOLMER/BROTHERSON LTD
ANDES/NEW YORK

Published by
WOOLMER/BROTHERSON LTD., ANDES, NEW YORK 13731
All rights reserved
First Printing

Grateful acknowledgment is made to the following publications where
many of these poems first appeared:

Aisling:	"The Missing."
Beloit Poetry Journal:	"The Uncomfortable Tic: To Robert Frost."
Between Two Worlds:	"One Always Asks."
Blue Unicorn:	"Domestic Sonnet: Unseparate."
Chicago Tribune:	"The Relative" and "Chicago Airport."
Mariner:	"The Outpost."
New World Writing:	"Fabliau For A Far-Flung Baby."
Peace and Pieces:	"On Driving Past Flowers And Having An Accident."
Poetry:	(some of these poems appeared in earlier versions) "Of Singles And Doubles," "Summer Camp: Wane," "Bird And Bell," "Easter Of The Mill," "Joy And The Presence Of Snakes," "The Enchantment," "Latin Lecturer: Last Class Before Summer," "Sun At Veracruz," "Poet As Bullfighter," "The Party," "Death Of The Story Teller," "Sea Look," "Quarrel," and "What He Sees."
Red Clay Reader:	"The Disease."
Saturday Review:	"American July" (called "Boy and Parade").
Southern Poetry Review:	"Letter To Belden."
Works:	"The Bird Watch" and "Wax Works."

"After The Storm" originally appeared in *Mark In Time,* edited by
Nick Harvey. Copyright © 1971 by Glide Publications.

CONTENTS

OF SINGLES AND DOUBLES

I

All clucks have loose shingles,
 Rasp their non-battering engines
 Feeding among themselves,
 Or shelves on shelves of selves,
 Their bed-feathers boost.

But gulls, the singles,
 Fly up from the coast like shalls.

Can you sustain this feather,
 Your sailboat's longing from blue to blue,
                or take
 A gull's cross-cut over the lots
 He loves?

                                        1952

The peripatetic stars without any longer
Their easeful hair;
The steppers over
The pepperwood.

Oh the people all are sleeping
Together as in a waltz.
Under the trees in cots
They idle their engines.

Away to the Hayward Hill the cars in pairs
Rise to a roar, wail—
Loose the wild country gone through:
Western billboard and buffalo
Leave to its fences.

And all night long without motor
The stars on the move:
Calypso, Juno, Gemini,
The former tenants, gone and handless—
Moved by the scenery movers and unvaulted
As seeds out of a new summer.

That pied priest who comes out of
Anything tearing its autumn up,
Wreaking its colors,
Is shaking his sleeves, is here.

Craig Ranch, Willits, 1948

If this were the only bird:
In the tree, chief planet—
Or half-way shade
Willow-raided and barred;

If this were the only song,
In the hand's chief platter
Cheep, cheese, or morsel sound:

His bucket down-sky of song
Reversed, donged,
To me, his anybody, his afternoon's wife's witness
Of bell without wrong, but ring
His gallon song.

His trillium time,
double in bloom,
ends my betweening.

A world of poles and poles
With the wires leaning . . . .
Housewives talk in meanings:

Shelling of peas, all of their pearls
Unstrung, and falling over-long
And well-flung, when suddenly
The telephone's Tel. & Tel.—
Cunning as code is, absolute
And fell as a prayer between gods

                who toss it,
Who laugh like larks and the prayer
Falls like a head.

                            1948

Where are my mother's brambles . . .
Her scarlet self, long gone?
O billboard growing larger
in her apron,
What airs bore me,
What Celtic and horneted language!

No harrow or stick to plough with,
No tool or shillelagh,
She had a tongue to dish up
Or diminish! . . . . And where was the man
Could regale her with a beasting? . . .
What bee-sting love unstickle
Her lasting frump?

That she should lie like a quilt
In the open, was all her fear—
Moon-watched,
The God-eye rolling.

Yet fluffed and unfeathered,
By child taken up:
Perjured but likewise honored,
Her Xmas-tree self, for once,
She was a ferris wheel
Of Catholic, queenly wares;
Roasters her hardware were
And collanders, and loud pots.

And the babies were real in their smells,
Cherubs to queen her . . .
She must make them always to last,
The dissolving candies . . . .

Any complainers shall burn
With her angry linaments,
                    who pinned
The saints in their wide
And flowery agonies
Over my bed and hers.

                                        1975

I

Take back your lambs, your lather,
Other whites this weather.

From the gatherers run,
Their millrace and hound
Roaring what sheep over what ground.

Hide. In the groves, garrets, cotes of eyes.
The pigeon puts his wing by elbowless,
Hens cut, cocks panic, gavot,
Leg clacking leg—
Rafters hung,
Groats lost.

And the sheep-kill happens steep
The sheep died sideways like moons.
Cloudy and stiff they float now
Without dalliance.

In barns they cry
The cock of all time is dead.
Karat his legs were of gold,
His spur, his spring;
And the pianos dropping their jewels for him till daylight,
The player, pushing her hands like carts
Their backs thick with garnet.

Easter. The slow-walking lambs go home,
The shorn go home. Takest home
Children only, not others
Of tool and horn?

I went by the old house and lot
Over by the abandoned airlines

Where winds come in like letters unmarked or mailed:
The mad unwalking old house
Never to rise up, vanish, or turn,
Its wires canceled, its birds,
Unwhistled by twig or carrier.

And the lady who was a lady,
The interpreter, who played the piano
Sidewise, they tell how
The dark fell out of her porches
All her carts of geranium overturned.
When she was gone the garrets
Played on and on after her.

At cock-sing she is carried out flat
Like a letter dressed for a box.
The clergy, drag of their tails,
The eggs in the wassail bowl.

When again shall death be
As posters of casual sheep
Or pastures of a Lord not returned?
Only in a sleeper's dream of a daylight.
And who shall say, rising or risen, I saw her
Come again but at cock-crow?

Let her sleep in her death-dress
Her virginity,
Her life an honorable mention.
Home, little moist myth,
Arisen away and preceding itself into heaven
With its detachment of quilts, cherubs, horrors,
And the residents of prayers.

II
Run sheep run sheep run of the mill,
For terrier death at heel,

For kill brighter than kindle to the mind that kills.

To the mind that kills. Kill:
Flower, fastness,
Red mill of a reason rampant,
Furious fair.

The Abraham who bends is not
That Abraham whose beard
Blows like a copper Lord's:
The new child glistens, is spared
At some cock-crow of God. Oh no,
Feel in your palm's soft padded axe
The sword.

The heart is by all means the grave.
What Lucy wears as locket, what hero
Offers to fear as door-lock is not:
But the terrible two-part engine,
Closet of self is heart.

III
The celebrant feast
To isolate the dead:
The disconnecting rituals.

We, the still living triumph,
Hearts open and shiny,
Seated as for a game—
All Knaves and Queens—
Guarded,
Certain as trumps.

> Remember: jails blow, locks hurt,
> posts pound, fists cram, pages
> burn;
> Rage the imprisoned dead
> Whom we seize as prisoners.

Turn not your face from me—
     a card's man:
Half an eye in a board house.
The journey not taken attacks
     my landscape,
The fingers and joints of post
Point no place I have been.

Coffin-indentured friend,
Future and enemy,
Easter rousts us
Out of the troddest places
Out of the palaces of tracked heel,
The wet brown dawn of the ground.

Any worm in its transit
Is my saviour:
The worm, my tyrant,
Blooms me.

And the green, springful eye of a man
Is full of the world that time:
Eyes in looks, in latches, at eve,
In sidle of room, in eye's heel of an eye.
And seeing, seeing: outspill of all
     one's rubies, leaving him
Robbed, reeded and remembered—
The broken charts, the chunks, the jaw-bones.
Celled, selved, and sold.
Halved and manied—
Fern-conscious, jew-dark, cudgel Spring.

I met in that country a cock,
Leg strong and touchy
As to help up an overload
Of Knight all feathers: his eye
Lighted by streets of treason,
Afraid of the rose,

But eye to stop you
Of gem, karat, or agent.

"Who guiltless comes upon immortal morning
Rides a pale horse; half-halts
In the parted wood, is patched
Of earlier greens, and bears
Like a man not born."

Guilt, my despite,
My violin close of kin,
Hermes and passenger.

The worm in the astonished corps
      impinges:
Knowledge like mercury
Spreads through the veins in a
      seizure.

Riddled with terrible questions,
Living its arrows,
          the body
Finds itself opal,
          is topical,
"I was splendid!"
Hums in the infant air:

Glows the completed life,
Loud as a fire.
The visible hearth sounds.

1949 and 1978

Joy is still the startle and sting.
No switch of attention, joy but to increase;
No flash of the serpent tail but sorrows cease
And perjury doesn't apply.

Are you ashamed to be so joyed and queer,
Turked and hen-cowered, serious as an egg?—
The fool of the golden garden in the glade
Hatching your far-flung finches cockle-wise,
Yourself the blunder—joke
Of the small and yellowish surprise?

Be not ashamed, not ashed; be you-stead, odd,
Fished as a sailor, boosted as a whale
That rides the solemns sideways and is god—
Lost as the sailor's envy in the sea,
Swinging its serpents singly or in three,
Swung by its own incorrigible tail.

To love anyway, no matter what mortal or coil:
Be lasted in the lands on lands of green:
Be lucky in the eyes on eyes of seas:

The birds shall lift the upper boughs like houris,
Their treble house
Shaking with shreds of weed,
                              and you recall
The decks of the ferry vacant,
The sun's increase
On Orpheus whose diametric feet
Scattered the serpents.
                              And the women struck
Who killed him blindly without any thought
Of music in his hearing, yet the plain
All rushed to the unintended side of rain.

Their ears were stopped with singing of the slain—
And apples in the offing yet to eat.

1953

THE ENCHANTMENT
for Bill

I

After the barking around the slaughter-house
Down at the bone-throw
And the evening seeping in troughs,
The stars begin their circuitous life of sheep.

The pointed lights
Circle the head of the dog
Folded and twitched,
The sleeper out of the race.

No man who runs as before a machine
From the star-flint in eyes,
From love the two-parts diamond,
Recalls justice or chiming.

Knowing hound-hollow,
He lengthens and follows—
Uttering sounds not his.

II

However we happen to be in these parallels,
And in spite of the people who keep asking us
"How do you sleep so well among the car lines?"—
Though the ears grow large, the Dutchmen fly,
And we sometimes dissemble,
Forgive us our fact, we are here.

By dark, the sounds grow long
And the fingers loom:
Love is no anteroom, love
Is the arrival and gong.

And ear to the ground that carries us,
Carries and marries: hard to the chest,

Those pipes in you most bold
Because they only guess—
And that tree whose branches mine are,
Bone for bone:
All of its leaves thrown,
Thrown, as away!

       How they stay,
Each socket and clove—
(The apparent stars do not fall)
How, after all, they stay.

                                        1950

FABLIAU FOR A FAR-FLUNG BABY

for Camas

I: *"She Seems to be Trying to Crawl. . ."*

She goes by herself, ferries,
Spills herself trying—
A model of creature not to be wound or sprung:
As a bird is, sweetly swung,
Not leaning, not lying,
Not quite swimming, not quite boating,
                     and not quite flying.

Arms, legs, spider together.
The touch is of feather—
Or burr, as her millionaire pleasure
Spends her. The eyes perch.

And all of the parent air cannot inclose
Her junket or her search,
Which begins, begins, and begins over:
None of the things she reaches for
                  are anywhere;
They hover.
             Were she in clover
She would mark it less than the weather.

Who is all she is,
Like a small bead:
She is autonomous, incompetent,
And adaptable as a wig,
Or capital of the state in summer
When the winds change speed
And the twilight in the counties
Turns the pigs,
And the stars grow big.

Who would weeds for her wear?
Dress as a girl in tears

And not have her? Who indeed.
Certainly not I, who her fortune told
In the flocked and feathered air.

II: *"She Seems to be Trying to Talk . . . "*

The sound unexpected,
Amalgam of lark and alarm—
She greets without any surprise
The elves and the thieves.

The elves and the thieves in air,
Counting their fingers,
Or bargaining higher on carpets,
Sifting and sifting.

Listen, the sounds of the sieve.

No hordes, no hounds, no horns we have;
We have a baby,
              and she is a fount of anger—
Oh, she is eloquent.

And the language of her belief,
Like a trout in stream,
Early and Arabic, flies like an arguer upward;
              And she after it,
Half-slipping and half-encountering
The espionage of dreams.

1954

(The students write in class)
I see them write . . . .
  Hair sweeping like native fern;
Like unmoved, approaching people,
Heads balancing the memorized diamonds.

I, in some measure, am steering their
        crowds of palms:
Feel close their instinctual movements.

I might say, "We are not permanent at
        this outpost:
You will divine a corollary landscape
        and a practice language,
Since nobody ever stays in the native village
Where he is, in fact, immortal—
And you are leaving yours."

The hills go down one by one
        in the plural evenings . . .
Who has not heard the gongs? . . . the suns
Come trembling disc by disc,
        and after dark
There hurls a starry bobbin . . . .

They watch on their strange verandahs;
Some barely see me, some
Recoil at my angry beads.

For some, a star
        as real as a land-raised apple
Is crowding their thinking
Onto those paper fields.

                    College of Marin, 1968

LATIN LECTURER:
LAST CLASS BEFORE SUMMER

Whatever his own eye troubles to make clear,
As the eagle plunges,
Ideal swimmer and angel,
He saw, and sees.

And the birds in his metaphors now
Are two-winged, ancient—
The feathers exact as shown
On the sides in dictionaries
With Roman triremes.
                          Ranting against the seasons,
He rails at his loss of ships.

He takes to himself his watch,
As the face of an elder—
Its shielded, impassioned wheel;
And feeling unsteady,
Senses the loss of his objects.

The lime and the envy burn
In transalpine snow;
The birds like jacks
Have tracked the plain and crossed it
And flown like nail-prints.

And the sunset comes over water:
Sets in a clutch of boughs
As a hen or vacancy:
And he knows, but loves, what he is.

Oh water, be under us like a shine.
The floor we played on,
The linoleum we paid for,
The life we led.

                                            1951

He waits, in a land where the daylight comes
                down to the ground
In air that is mowed and empty
                with only
The smell of the waterfalls of alfalfa,
When the waves begin swelling
Then roll and increase like drums.

A butterfly moves its wings
With the light hustle of hay;
The flag is farther—
Basted by a breeze.

Now as from dark to light
The bunting catches the flares—
Air full of criers,
Flag flying its sentence:

And he preens with belief,
                seeing
The pigeons battle the sunlight,
Rising on higher airs—
The dark ring at the throat
Shining and sailing,
The ring on the foot
Like a light.

And at night the true-blue boy stays on
As long as the fire works or lasts,
And in September remembers,
Sitting among the runes, faced with the
                numbers:
Sees that the fractions sprout,
Multiply leg and wing,
And the boy laughs out
As the grasshoppers jump like fire.

1956

THE RELATIVE

Vincent van Gogh, it is the year's resolve
To speak in me the relative who knows,
Though all revolves . . . the fields, the skies, the crows . . .
That all the moving climates are not love;

Who sees the summers breaking act by act,
The fruit trees thickening to a foaming roar,
The branches lifting oar after oar after oar,
Who does not love that blossoming cataract.

Reluctant lovers; where are the *little* powers
For what in us the seasons cannot serve,
Who fly from the too-much we don't deserve
To any desert we can think is ours?

Vincent, how is it, now, that you're the one
We wait for like unrung bells? Your wrinkling fields
Thicken the heart; whatever the look will yield
We crack our eyes to squint into your sun:

You crossed the place for us with blacker birds
Than any waves of wheat have lately worn.
The fields you could not enter, bright with scorn,
Are beautiful, and charge me with these words.

1969

The plane comes in like a tern
    then hesitates
With turnabout of ten hens,
    the motors
Uttering our failure and lust to arrive.

The shells we collected
To immunize thought on returning
Sting now at neck or sleeve.

What if those meeting us falter,
    or fail to seem
The remnants of what we remembered?
An engine's cough is making us cold
    in the pipelines,
Our wings contracting like elbows.

So any returner is coasting the rocks
    and the maps:
Dreading at half-moon, fearing
His love of country;
And he dreams as a crossed harp
Home, and the shaking weeds:

Till the sights go under,
Sliding us from our vanities;
The lights come on like residents.

Return is a small, tough fawn.

1967

One always asks, "Who are these people?"
Though the sun plates them
And the pools show openly in their eyes
Like good intentions:

Though their dogs, leg-deep in the rusted gardens,
Are basking like trucks;
While the new-born motors, their lineaments'
                              true loves,
Wax and revolve like Venuses:

Though their talk into telephones
Turns as a mountain beautiful,
Leaves a calypso shape on the hung-out air:

Yet all they ever speak of are the deer,
Speak guiltily, as of a burning.
When the dusk turns bright its quills,
And the dark comes up on the walls
To the line of the question,

Not frightening any children, but
                              some musicians
Who have come to feel lately that trumpets,
                              even played singly,
Are somehow unfortunate, heralding back
                              to a time
When hunting was not an evil
And required no license.

And the women with children on the ends
                              of their hands
Like kite-tails, draw them indoors,
Saying a prayer for his lordship:

Who has lately pointed out how all our worship
Depends on a loss of heat:

It revolves around the sun like an aversion,
And glows as the sun declines.

                                        1960

Land of the lorded stone
And libertied crab, let us stay
Till the mind moves in its surf
To the colors of days and times
And houses yellow with meal,
And blue looking out at doors,
And time by melon, the sky
Not halved, quartered, or blinked
But in thinking
"The crab meddles and moves."

By moon the sand's wet picture
Under the palm's wheel.

At noon the ocean flying with hats;
The windows, sheets to the draft
And ships in the eyes.

The distance is white and hard
And site of the shark.
Mover of ships and remover,
Sea without side;
The tropic absolute stare
Is the fish of brass,
Is the seizer.

The sun that belonged to Cortéz, Señor,
                            is yours.
Sky without shield
But his.

1950

This lingual Spanish brocade, O this
               light's veronica.
Amanuensis of heat, and the sun's chief actor—
Step after step in that pigment
To burn his beholder:
No stair augments his honor,
Or his word.

Takes like a sword his meaning to the beast
That neither reports nor learns—
               by clotted hoof, or by kelp-dark,
               bent, wound-widening heart—
The colors to lift or retract.

Till performance bursting and singeing,
The carrying trumpets
Mock seaward.
And the tongues and racks of sea
Permit no language.

Art thou at odds with the fringes?
The hooking foam?

What appears in fingers and figures?—
But none lovable,
As only the sea can countersign
               love,
Or a wound.

                                                1961

Do not assume enmity, sitting among the generals,
Their brass stares
Galvanizing day:

The chalk light ages you,
Lips wrinkling the stones:
As eye to eye we turn with the whiteness of statues—
Seeing, uncentered, the celebrated face,
        not ours,
And always unended by death.

Whatever difference or peace there is between us,
Like the crevice in rock,
I will salute as the glitter in lilies.

Let us go forth, the
Membrane of cold at kiss,
Its courteous touch
No accident.
Hands on the pillars
        as hands on the heads of dwarves,
Footfall on stair,
We are no more odd than our efforts.

Though we learn to speak with a muscle of tongue
        that can wrestle an angel even while it changes,
Shall we never speak of ourselves?

Collaboration is a form of jealousy in which
What you own, and what you do not own,
Forever remains unclear,
And there is no question as to what you love.

                        1963

In any roomful
The people are the abstractions,
The pockets of burned-out hearts.

Eyes on their jags of enemies
Range the pianos of sense.
The lights come on like little animals.

Who spoke here first
Are gone from the windows'
Colors and jars.

Who spoke here first as originals
Their blared, unforgettable dialect
Now speak through the pin-killing glass.

I have seen the asthmatic, personal lights
              of a mansion
The private cough like a flower,
Tipple and leave in the starry, garrulous walks.

The camels no longer used by the rich and witty
Fetch in the distance;
And our good fortune, like the distinct whereabouts
Of the ibex or pterodactyl, not certain:

We have failed like mastiffs
To master the birds' positions—
The joke after joke in the leaves:

And failing is part of the shine,
And all of the enmity.

                                        1959

OF SINGLES AND DOUBLES
II

Beware of the amber error that is love,
Amber and mass of its continent,
And of all the connecting errors which make
            wandering lovable:

Though you glare with the volume
And lethargy of a head,
Though the bird escape, and that disc
That was going to be your fame:
"You shall not leave me for mortal."

Some eyes look up to our windows,
The quails of courtesy in them,
Or watch with a calmness of cannisters
Our morals passing like diamonds.

Though you perish in saying of speeches
Sainted in your own eyes
For all the terrible animals
That come into your eyes like ingots,

Yet here is the cracking of the bears
                  of our fears,
The continent and darker hiding
Than self or other vertebrate.

                                          1963

But being alone is nothing you can seek
Without much to resolve that is felt
In its weight like statues; or kept in their
Lawns of sleep by the old and fruitful.

When the dust sifts spot by spot on our
Natures, and the half-leaf tarnishes,
We abandon life for what we were assigned to,
Amid peelings of sun and citrus.

So take your place into my thought
And inherited hall with the amiable
Assurance of a question unanswered
And a dry wrinkling of candles,

Not focusing the day's blue cannon and wobble
And not hearing the mountains, rack behind rack.

1955

Faced with the other face, and the water
Clearing it:
As a city surprised by desertion
My face spilled little by little
In every candor,
My heart in every wanderer.

And the Argo was deeply in debt to its witch,
Not knowing whether to turn back
Or carry on the dark woman:
Her hand upraised,
Her art in the air like a hollyhock.

But I am not Medea,
The betrayal modern—
Even to me elusive,
Involving no murderers.

Wishing to be consummately ordinary,
Enchantment happens anyway . . .

In a Monday's blue wash
I see the surfacing phantom
Ghosting the yard—
The clothesline going full tilt,
The blowing sleeves without arms.

I grow envious of stippled sleep—
The mindless slope
Where words arise to control
Like lovers, but not loving:

Sink to the watery leagues,
The long, low latitudes:
In dream the imagined presence
Strong and wild.

The art that creates
Can harden the heart like an emerald,
Missing the living face.

In its wake, our ship
Is scribbling some lines on water:
Grief of the loss, the irretrievable
Identities gone under as we change,
As the necessary links
Unloose like hands:
The sea takes our reasons.

1954 and 1978

So near we came to disaster
In walking the skin-dark water:
I remember as a procession of crowned
                    invisible blacks
The king-like encounter with custom
And your countenance.

Met by wildness,
The life I had thought of vanishes.
Your proffered hand
Touched the essential choice.

Easily, under the century-hoarding
                    rains:
The springing snakes of the long
Unwinding summer.
The senses disconnect
And all pasts codify.

In such dark climate
Where even the hunchbacked orchids
Are invited to stay . . .
                    odor of tropics . . . .
The beasts of burden subtle:
Embarrassment is a gift of ebony
                    and bright fruit,
An unexpected tallness
Toppling the sun.

Even so short a safari as mine
Into primitive clarity
Connects the memory with
A long and spacious willfulness
Of savannahs.

Love—sometimes unwanted—

Yet is without reserve.
Whole strangeness.
While at home, the old familiars
Haggle with presence.

Returning is more difficult.
I cannot keep Sundays, bake,
Be conjugal.
         A foreign joy
Has entered the cauldrons.

1961

Your presence, like memory raising its grand device
Makes everything leap in its margins;
Language, that continuous meadow flourishes;
Enjoy in the mouth
The rinse of the world-wide wording.

Makers of all ways glorious and flood-like,
Of cities fair in their limits
With sunrise at morning lighting
The sharp discernment of hills:
You let me release my accostable island,
My most furious possession
To go with the sea-moved powers:
          O myopic angel
And master of movable forms.

1961

for Charles Orgibet

The air opening and closing, never shutting,
        its brilliant bellows
Collects our lives,

And the brain's dolphin's clavichord
Brings some consent not ours
To the mind that pricks and retains
Like a spice's presence
Its few dark cloves.

To him who looks everywhere,
Seeing his natural answer:
In the fern a fern, in the leaf a leaf—
Form without flower or peril—
And in the sun
As stunned by the fir-dark light,
Through many climates and errors,
Sees again:
Remarks upon each for its particular *would,*
Its fresh collapsible bird.

Touching each with a rod,
Sees like a sawyer eternal life
In an odd and removable portion
Between the fingers of water.

Where the water parts from the hand
        without parting:
The small leaves everywhere,
The small pieces of water:
The man walks flawlessly shaped,
And his face is stiff with love.

1965

ON DRIVING PAST FLOWERS
AND HAVING AN ACCIDENT

They crash on our spotted sight
Like magnificent blood
While our windshield moves its stiff window:

Around and around the block
To retract the mood
Of flowers that direct us
Like floods.

How is it possible for me to
Speak to my dead-right passenger
And fly from the presence of
These sky-stead objects?

The windshield is moving its view
Lest much be true
That does not report its light
Yet blossoms sight.

No galaxies surprise us like those that cut,
And then dissolve,
Leaving appearance unaided.

So Galileo, condemned because of the planets,
Is searching the salt-bright ground
Of his final prison,
And we our scarred palms.

There is more to a life
Than a sentence, and a long last-look:

We cannot reflock our thinking
In these times without Eros.
The flowers correct the error
We never see.

1962

DEATH OF THE STORY TELLER
for Bill

The cat is a charmer:
Its stiff ruffles
Clarify like dandelions
The sunlight's bauble of land;
As daylight arrives like a splendid,
    embarrassed connection
Between trees' deep dark
And the upswinging, murmurous lawns.

And the story-teller returns to his own country,
Taking the heart-shapes with him.
He wades with their caskets into interior hills;
And the underground lake—his legion and
    honor—without vanishing,
Spreads like a risk
Forgiveness and truth for his story:
Among insolent arts of the walls that are
    pocked with his name.

           1964

Along the streaming ground, the wet leaves
          fit like fish
And shine like talk.
The prints of xylophone horses
Clang and revise
Their clear and candid marks.

And only a funeral under a tall quartz sky
Can bring us together as steeply
As these oak trees
And this tomb.

All talk seems genuine: the syllables make evident
Their wild, pronounced colonies.

The word is out—a racket of hail and rhyme
Is landing a few Greek letters at a time.

If any have other knowledge of the crime,
Let him speak, lest the privilege harden;
Let us acknowledge
The rains were heavy and the damage severe—

Yet there are times when the uncut universe comes close
And whets like a diamond;

That the privacy of clarity emerge,
And the useful joy seem near.

And the diamond is odd in its meaning;
It rests in its water-mark;
Is read by the shining door.

                                        1965

In the focal sun,
The soul is snapping its locket.
Find by the shore, by the clam-clanging,
                    clarion tides,
By shells, by periwinkles, by urchins reveled,
How the thousand on thousand lives
Let down their gear.

Star of a tide-pool's genius; hear
                    far out
The many-minding horses turn on their
                    marks.
Listen and feel
Their clippeting arcs' far hearts.

1964

THE UNCOMFORTABLE TIC:
TO ROBERT FROST

If you were there to see the moon blow through—
The clouds blotting and fetching, finally going—
Still, if you saw the blowing, you will know
How much of moonlight you might misconstrue:
Who can foretell, autumns and crows away,
What a slow switch of bough goes on to say?

Imagining it right,
Even without the sleight
Of looking the other way,
Frost: hoeing, pruning, patching, conserving,
                   and weather-forecasting,
Knows otherwise.

To see as they shine with sunlight and with salt
The feathers, the bird's marauders,
Yellows and red;
To see the dead tree dead;
To think while the world wages.

To bob for apples,
Fallways to go down
(And you can only fall . . .)
Tearing the pages:

And then to see the crippled tree blow up,
Blow like a chariot, dragging the slow swing,
Dragging the field to southward, everything leaving:
And then to know by the twitch in the eye of joy—
The uncomfortable tic—
Another Spring,
Another race for it.

                                   1957

I broke out in really-trues;
My toes became nobles.
Ill at ease, joyful, and fully aware
How some of the doorknobs are booming
With the authority of promoted toads,
I better announce myself.

Though I am thirteen and a virgin,
Though the daylight is thin as an errand,
Though the new-born windows (not matching
            their excellent frames)
Are full to excess with their
Clear and banging views,
I better start out.

No King of Circumstance or Queen of Chance
Can alter my marvel: which is, indeed
To be odd. Am I not the odd one,
The node to a wilderness?

As if all of the elk of the world
Are walking a skyful of antlers,
Their lives extending from their heads of leaves.

And that balancing holly
Is all of the system I need.

1970

The bird in the spray like a turning boy:
His vision is beaded and hilly
But his time-sense regular.
We watch him pivot,
Steering his palace of drops . . . .
Though each drop were a fallacy,
He still could be true:
And loved, as a rose
Is valued for its scars.

Truant, rapacious, and loud,
His clock his sound, his time
Surrounds him . . .
He only has to fly,
We have to decide;

Not sure of our lasting peace,
                we imagine
The waver in us to be flight.

For those who decide to dwell in themselves
                only long enough
To say farewell to each special occasion,
The bird revokes like a chime.

But there are others, since Chaucer, for whom
His meaning and triviality are profound.
These are the ones for whom an alarm going off
Will strike at their fears like a
Partial hope of heaven: and for them
Nothing can make heretical his play:

He sings in the open
His shattering, rainable bars . . . .

                                        1968

LETTER TO BELDEN
for Sheldon Barrett

In St. Louis as at Fontainbleau there is
A park too large to walk in,
Where welcome becomes a handicap.
The police on guard,
A patch on each heart like a trump:
They smile, I walk,
I wear myself out saying thank you.

And you, no thanks to you,
Belden my enemy—
You married my daughter
You shifter of weights and loves,
Now among peacocks and apes
        I wander,
Expecting wonders, deserving
          homage.

The zoo gives none,
Not the pelican's loose beak
And unhindered eye.
An alligator's beveled mass slides off
Like a discarded purse.

The cabarets that worked so well by gaslight
Do not delight me now:
Nudge of the searchlights,
Bulb after flaring bulb,
And each one telling
That I am this horrible light show.

Or markets in passing,
The meat in the showcases elderly;
The raw dead Sundays;
The ghettos of grieving windows.
And those, with their chattel,
Whose faces are watching like lanterns.

And you, no thanks to you, Belden

my enemy.
Your job—to dispossess, in the
       heat of the day:
Wrenching the white refrigerators
       hoarsely
Onto the movable dollies.

The blacks are moving, and
The clairvoyant stain:
They are pulling their shadows out
Like the wings of doves.

It is more than absence,
More than abandonment,
More than love gone elsewhere.
It comes up under the sidewalks
And shatters the city.
The shutters are drawn,
But the air is still strong as a carnival.

We serve what we understand,
But what we fail to,
We love like a passionate answer.

In the town where the traffic
Is turning itself to jazz,
And the jays take off from the sound
Like devisive brooms,
Is a statue of Louis,
The patron saint of this city.

Pass without notice,
Missourians, eaters of lard.

Perhaps the Missouri I despise
Has its cardinal uses,
And the King, who was never here,
Has nothing to say.

                              1968

THE SANCHEZ ADOBE
for the Turriettas

Department of California Monuments
Hours: 1-4, 10-12
Closed Thanksgiving,
Christmas & New Year's

Near the highway stands the old adobe
The hemlocks drifting its porches like dry rain.

There is no well here. I am shucked
By the gallant Spanish.

Out in the chalky glare,
                in the brassbound sunlight
. . . . A dipper hung here,
                studded with drops like hearts,
The wet tin thronging my hands with cold.

We who dispossessed them have rights also—
Who come, helpless as voyeurs—their meanings
Still on our eyelids like stale sunflowers,
Our hands turning to braille.

Why do I have to be the one who is colorless,
Revealed in the granular courtyard,
While their strong buckets
Are knocking like untongued bells?

Dreading to say,
. . . . "It is a form of love.
                These Spanish envoys
Bent us to all we know of the courtly dances.
Their civil rites so calculated as to
Complicate and enhance beauty,
                their proliferating arbors
Became us, for we thought of them as leaves."

I disagree with my heart,

And resume travel.

A bird flies by on one wing
Like a narrow soldier.

I wave in profile,
An important statue.

I who was always in their futures
Like rain.

1974

Solid the bird that wavers the
            carolling bush:
Whine of a bell—our fortune
            which is
Cracked and considerate:

And I feel, as the moment of a
            beast's change,
The Autumn strike, full of streaks.

By candle we notice
The bird's yellow and burn.
When he flies, he carries his wings
In the wind like plaids.

When the necessary, loved hand
Grows transparent . . .
Lifts its twig . . .
When the winter,
Loosed from its virginal glare
Floods us with brine;
When the sun is freed from its mill
Where it glowed like a sweltering ox—
We weep, we accept the time.

At middle age, and indoors
We fathom impending evening.
The twilight is balancing the
Dappled enormous meadows
And clear cows.

We watch with impatience and wealth
Our children, the advancing
            strangers.

Briefly the village is lighted by
            its creeks:

From roll of the surf,
The roses evolve like chargers,
And we pick up the morning
As facing an excellent shell.

1963

POEM FOR THE FIFTIES
for my daughters

I

We were the wheelers of carts.
We carried layers of weather
On our skins like samples:
Sailed through the canyons of cans
With seductive labels
Telling us what we want:
The compulsive marrieds.

Pregnant, remember, we wore
Our bellies like badges,
We resonated to the happy cans.
Ours was the era of the friendly
                    policeman:
God as my enemy was not so right
As these orderlies—
                    no library stacks
So venal as this whole hunger for love:
The coming of age of conformity,
We would do anything
To preserve our favorite brands.

Our vouchers were babies
Lovely as ferns at weddings.
In Supermarkets we dreamed
Through the channel aisles,
                    our baskets
Off-springing with life.

But the children,
Alert in their hinges,
Were riding the rails.
We pushed, they traveled.

II
I can recall
In hammered-out old parks
How we were exposed
For the slow toads that we are.

The children, their lusty colors
Recharging vision, and passing
Some steaming fountain's
Sexless rage, foreign to us
As Mexico or as Persia . . .
Embarrassed our dry talk,
Interior oil-wells filling,
The fat crawling with fear
To be so alive.

I have heard chatterers—
Scatter-birds or children,
Chop up the evenest morning
With their axes:
Tear us like posters,
Starting us from our originals.

For they bloom, they do bloom,
The passengers in the carts.
We could only helplessly trail
Those through whom we could foresee:
Our disaster-purchasers,
Our grave results.

So hold most dear to the young,
Whom to hold most dear
Is ludicrous as skin to wear,
And I like a fur-bearing animal:

Dissolution to them is not horrible,
Not seen as an aging face . . . .

They rustle, make palpable dust
In just walking or flying.

At adolescence they disappear
To roust in a stevedore's morning . . .
Leaving to look at,
Old cars.
                    They reappear
In the words you write at the last.

To my hand comes a movement
Of fern, or print of an old coin
Sad with the face of some President
Or Caesar.
                    Not hoping for storm
Like someone who can't shed tears,
The wet rain lands
And I feel with my leather face.

III
I have wandered through the shelves on
                    shelves without legend
Trying to live by reading the deadly
                    directions:
The bread pre-baked, yet holy, the
                    cakes, the rebates,
The untouched, Immaculate I,
The just desserts.

No glance from the hero's
Winning side of the package,
No cubit added,
Nothing for comfort but coupons.

The awkward length of my wings
Makes flight unsupportable:
There is too much craft to take off

From these narrow canyons,
But the winds are changing directions.

Now I sign my name singly
As in writing a will or pardon:
My signature, that favored and
            graceless spider
Leaving all the account of a marriage
That there is.

Until sorting possessions, and holding
Some darling vase in my hands
Like a head, I think of my daughter's
Small, indivisible robin's egg of a face,
Learned and leaved, as sparrows
Were there alight . . . .

Then there's all that flowering,
Clear as a printed cloth,
That Spring does—
The blossoming faces,
Print after Florentine print,
With all of us turning the colors
Of garrulous Persians:

Reveals some life not ours to give,
            yet we give it—
(Shall I enchoke my rage? Dispense
            it like gold?)

And my flying carpet, invention, is
            still working its fringes:
The fabric is worn, but it shakes the nose
            like acacia,
The rug flacking paisley and golden
            its sheaves on sheaves of dust
As it shakes out—shakes out—shakes out—

                                    1978

for Peter Gray

Through this filled universe at length we moved,
And did not move . . . the thick day bearing us.
There came an island pushing out of whiteness:
Blue to look up and see it, and to leave it
Was to watch darkness going out.

                             And next,
The fog backing the bridge: making it solid—
No sky-spring anywhere between the wires.

Peter said, "Fog is weather you can see,"
And breaking off from fog
As words from mind,
There were the sea birds
Bringing their bright beaks toward us.

                                        1941